A LOOK INSIDE
JOURNEY TO A HEALTHY SELF

TERRIE A. ALEXANDER

ME
WE

MORE EXCELLENT
WAY ENTERPRISES

Scripture references are taken from the King James Version and other versions of the Holy Bible.
Pronouns for referring to the Father, Son and Holy Spirit are capitalized intentionally and the words satan and devil are never capitalized.

Publisher:
More Excellent Way Enterprises
www.mewellc.com

First Edition
ISBN: 978-0-9864235-8-1

Library of Congress Control Number: 2016917118

Printed in the United States of America.

I dedicate this work to my family. To my husband of 34 years, Ruben A Alexander. He has always been a source of encouragement to me and was instrumental in helping me realize, through all I was dealing with, he really could not help me but it was an "inside job." To my eldest, Ruben G., my daughter in love, Alisha, and first grandchild, little Sarai, thank you. To my daughters Justine, who listened to me over and over and helped me in ways she cannot imagine and Jessica, who pushed me to give more when I thought I had given all I had.

TABLE OF CONTENTS

TABLE OF CONTENTS (CONT.)

FOREWORD

Genesis 2:7 says, *"And the Lord God formed man of the dust of the ground and breathed into his nostrils the breath of life; and man and became a living soul.. And the Lord God planted a garden … and there He put man whom He had formed."*

Relationships were created by God. The first healthy relationship started with God in the garden. However you cannot possibly have a healthy relationship with Him if you do not know who God is and who you are. In the forthcoming pages, Mrs. Alexander will share some wisdom in order to have a healthy relationship first with yourself. She will walk us through the pages of this book to help us understand ourselves better, take responsibility for our outcomes and develop and sustain healthy relationships with others. The adversary comes to kill, steal and destroy, and the first thing that he tries to destroy is your perception of yourself. God formed you. He created man in His very own image. The enemy is out to tell you that you are nothing, were nothing and will always be nothing. Typically, he does a pretty good job of convincing us of these erroneous opinions of ourselves. The enemy has the ability to completely obliterate us of our good self-image and make us feel hopeless without a healthy relationship with the Creator and ourselves. But the Lord declares that we are more than conquers through Christ Jesus.

We should give thanks for the relationships that God has placed in our paths. Sometimes we do not fully understand the impact relationships have on our lives. Several years ago, a man gave a word on relationships and said, "Everybody that you meet and every person that you have a relationship with whether past or present, that person's relationship with you will continue forever." That statement rings with truth because oftentimes we are not aware of how relationships affect us and how our self-image affects our interactions with others.

It is crucial that we have good relationships with each other. The Bible emphasizes that we should support the weak, be patient towards all men…that none render evil for evil unto any man. (See 1 Thessalonians 5:14-15). We are to support and do for those who are not able to do for themselves. This is not a revelation to suppress you or to discourage you. The Word, pertaining to relationships, is meant to encourage, uplift and to take you to new levels.

We have to encourage healthy relationships all around us. If I see my brother and my sister in a relationship that is moving south, then, out of love, I must go and undergird them and love them through their times of adversity, instead of talking the situation into the ground, saying things like, "*I knew it wouldn't work anyway.*" Whether at home, in the community or the workplace, all relationships are important. We should strive to make them healthy and keep them healthy.

In the Bible, Judea symbolizes the workplace (See Acts1:8). It is a community outside of the home. It is easy for us to keep the workplace out of the picture when talking about building meaningful rapports. Some people go to work and say, "I only talk to these folks because I have to. I'm here to work, get a paycheck, and be gone." But who knows what could come out of workplace relationships? The Word tells us to work as unto God and not unto men. God trusts you to be in the right place at the right time, doing the right thing in order to build strong relationships.

As an employer, I have to use my work to build relationships. I know when folks are faking. I see what they are doing. Sometimes you try to give them an opportunity to do the right thing the right way and it does not always work out. When it doesn't work out, there are consequences. That is how God is with us in our relationship with Him. He gives us an opportunity to do the right thing the right way. Integrity is paramount when building strong relationships. God is looking at integrity and character in all of us because we never know when people are looking at us.

A close friend of mine once told me that when I go into a room, I am a game changer. I change the atmosphere because of the Christ in me. And when I go places, because of my relationship with God, fellow men and with my family, I walk in favor.

We should walk in favor and be relational on every level – in the community, on the worldwide spectrum, in business and in marriage.

God will direct you in relationships that will produce favor, seeing that you have been faithful over the little challenges. If you have been faithful and have shown integrity in the workplace, in business endeavors, and in your marriage, God will make provisions for you. God will create changes in environments, which can create changes in the hearts of men that they may want to provide you with opportunities; therefore, building relationships.

We must understand that our relationship with God is first and foremost. You must understand that you are not complete in yourself, but you are complete with the Creator of creation through Christ Jesus. When you have a relationship with Him, only then can you begin to have a healthy relationship with mankind. You can begin to have a good relationship at home, in the workplace, in business and even with yourself when you begin to take "a look inside."

Elder Ruben A. Alexander, PA-C

INTRODUCTION

Throughout my life, I have spent a considerable amount of time searching for answers in my career, business, marriage and family. Like most, I sought after fulfillment and personal gratification. From my earliest of memories, I had everything going my way. I finished high school where I had been very popular; I was awarded a partial scholarship for college and I even graduated from there with honors.

Despite these victories, I did not like myself nor did I enjoy the company of those who surrounded me. I had friends and was dating a great guy who really cared for me. I had big dreams for the future that seemed within reach. Yet a happy, fulfilled life was something that continually evaded me. Something was missing.

When I accepted Jesus Christ as my Lord and Savior, I took strength and courage in the Holy Bible, *"For I know the thoughts that I think toward you, saith the Lord, thoughts of peace, and not of evil, to give you an expected end. Then shall ye call upon me, and ye shall go and pray unto me, and I will hearken unto you. And ye shall seek me, and find me, when ye shall search for me with all your heart"* (Jeremiah 29:11-13). I began a journey to find acceptance, happiness and love in this world.

By achieving personal fulfillment and gratification, it has become my utmost desire to help both the young and old attain the same. The purpose of my writing here is to help you save time, effort, and energy by avoiding looking in the wrong places in life for fulfillment. The book of John clearly tells us that *"If ye keep my commandments, ye shall abide in my love; even as I have kept my Father's commandments, and abide in his love. These things have I spoken unto you, that my joy might remain in you, and that your joy might be full"* (John 15:10-11).

I want the young ones to avoid life's pitfalls so that they can discover the true meaning of life at this early stage and the old ones to also make good use of their valuable time so that they can make a difference in this world and experience feelings of purpose.

As children of God, it is imperative that we have an accurate understanding of the different types of relationships that exist. Most people only focus on their relationship with God and with others, but having a healthy relationship with yourself first is crucial to the success of relationships with others. Besides, you're with yourself 100% of the time and if you do not like yourself, how can you expect any relationship or achievement to be happy, healthy, and fulfilling?

At the center of every relationship is 'you.' The great philosopher, Yogi Bear, said, *"Everywhere I go there I am."* This shows you cannot escape you, so, you ought to like you. But, God is so good that even if you do not like yourself, He has a solution to every problem. If you're a born-again believer, He came to live on the inside of you, and He won't leave you like He found you. If you cooperate with His promptings to grow, to develop and to change, you will be a better version of you, and that's really what it's about.

My passion regarding this derives from the fact that God has brought me from being a child and young adult with low self-esteem and all kinds of negativity, to a still-developing woman, truly growing gracefully.

I thank God for the Word of God. I thank God for salvation. I thank God for men and women of God who teach the Word. Also, I thank God that He saw fit never to leave me alone until I yielded and now I give Him thanks. Even after I came to Him and became a born-again believer, He never let me go. He continued to work on me until I recognized and realized who I was in Him, and it brought me to the place where I have more confidence today.

Physicians take X-rays to find out what's making our back, neck, or stomach hurt. They take an MRI to determine what may be causing the excruciating pain in a certain part of our body. They use an EKG to measure the rhythms of our heart. They take ultrasounds to see how a baby is growing inside of a woman. They use many other diagnostic tests to determine what ails us on the inside. We too need to take a look inside to know what is causing the emotional pain we feel and what is driving how we behave. With God's help, we have to remove those things that are not in line with what He says about us in His Word and believe that He desires for us to experience unspeakable joy and victorious living.

As a mature adult now, I can see so clearly what was dim in my earlier years. Life is beautiful and well worth experiencing. I understand that God has placed in me treasure to be mined by others for their growth, development and enjoyment. I was put on the earth to serve others and honor God. He has so richly blessed me and I will forever praise Him and be grateful. I could have been forever lost, but He saw fit to find me and use me for His glory!

Terrie A. Alexander

CHAPTER 1

HOW TO RELATE TO
YOURSELF

My life, after leaving my parent's home, began with equal parts of fear, trepidation, excitement and hope for the future. Deep down I always felt that life would be better than how I grew up, but I never realized my thinking was the root of my displeasure with the world around me.

"When you die, others who think they know you, will concoct things about you... Better pick up a pen and write it yourself, for you know yourself best."

Sholom Aleichem

I had to consider what I thought of myself, although at the time, I was unaware how vital it was to alter and improve my self-image. As I moved into adulthood, I was around people who did not necessarily lift me; people who meant well, but were not lifters.

When you think of how an airplane is propelled forward, there are four main qualities: lift, thrust, weight and drag. For the airplane, they serve a purpose to get the plane off the ground and into the air and keep it in motion. The same can be said for relationships; you do not need people who drag or weigh you down, you need folks who lift and help thrust you forward and encourage you to achieve goals.

One of the most common hindrances to reaching goals and living a life of fulfilment and fruitfulness is how we relate to ourselves.

In the Garden of Eden, the serpent succeeded in convincing our first parents that they were less than they could be. He pointed to the Creator as if He had deprived them of the knowledge they needed to be equal to God Himself. That lie, once believed, gave them a sense of inferiority. Once acted upon, the lie produced guilt and shame – so much so that they tried to hide themselves from the Lord. It also produced the first conflict between a man and wife.

Our understanding of ourselves is warped by false ideas about our self-worth and self-image. Presidents and paupers share those same struggles. False beliefs about yourself can rob you of relationships and opportunities to serve within God's kingdom.

What Do You Think of Yourself?

What do you think of yourself? What is the driving force behind those thoughts? When I was young, I had voices in my head incessantly telling me I was not good enough. Those voices stemmed from being told often that I was "black" (when black was not beautiful and black lives did not matter). I was constantly told that my neck was too long and my hair was too short and that I looked like an "ole African."

Those very words constructed images in my mind that were less than desirable. My self-image was warped by negative comments coming from parents and siblings who truly didn't know any better.

The old adage "sticks and stones may break my bones, but words could never hurt me" is the farthest thing from the truth. Words hold great power, no matter the speaker's intentions. In time, the words spoken to me shaped my thinking about myself. Because of them, I was always trying to disprove something. While these words made me stronger in the long run, they created feelings of disconnection within myself. I knew them to be false, but for many years to come I still entertained the notion that I was somehow lesser.

Do not think of yourself as a small, compressed, suffering thing. Think of yourself as graceful and expanding, no matter how unlikely it may seem at the time. - B.K.S. Iyengar

Life's pleasures seemed to escape me because I never felt worthy of anything good. How could I? All the negatives spoken over me had convinced me I was worthless. Things were being said like, "You'll never amount to anything. You are going to hit skid row," or "You'll just be a bum." These words became daily mantras that flowed throughout my household. Without realizing it, these words had taken ahold of me; they shaped my thinking, bogged down my self-esteem, and like a slow-acting poison, began destroying me and my relationships with others.

What people think of themselves has tremendous power over them and those with whom they come in contact. If you think you are a "bad, unworthy person," you will reason that anyone wanting to be a friend or showing an interest in you must not be worth very much either. An examination of the way you view yourself, your thoughts, your feelings, and your emotions should be heavily scrutinized on your way to being healthy.

Often times, my surroundings tried to dictate my thoughts. I grew up in an impoverished neighborhood. I often sat on the back porch and watched some of the boys in the nearby apartments sniff glue in a brown paper bag to get "high." They were trying to escape the ruined world they found themselves in. Life was often dismal, and they felt like there was no way out. There was a lot of teenage pregnancies, high school dropouts and violence in the neighborhood. Life looked hopeless.

If we believe in something bigger, there is an escape provided by our Lord (See 1 Corinthians 10:13). There is no such thing as an irresistible temptation. Though certainly, if we view each other through the wrong lens, we can be distracted by outward appearances. This is a terrible tragedy, because what is most valuable cannot be seen with our eyes. God looks at our hearts (See 1 Samuel 16:7) and knows the truth. To see truth is to not see with our eyes, but with the proper lens: our hearts.

The Lord has a surprise for those of you who have a world-warped self-image. In Ephesians 2:10, the Apostle Paul wrote, *"For we are his workmanship, created in Christ Jesus unto good works..."* Under the inspiration of God's Holy Spirit, the apostle described us as God's "workmanship." In modern English, this word literally means "masterpiece." You are God's masterpiece!

With the wrong mindset, you cannot see the masterpiece you are and those around you may not appreciate your inner value because they cannot see beyond the surface. Years ago, a teacher from Illinois explained that we look into a mirror and see less than we should. We do not see the masterpiece, but only the frame that surrounds it. Do not make that mistake!

I thank God that I was a fighter by nature, because when I looked into the mirror, I saw a dim view of the masterpiece I was. I did not allow myself to get caught up in the pressures of my surroundings. Something inside always told me I did not have to accept what I saw or what people told me. As a child, if there was something I wanted to do, I would ask for permission. My mother would challenge me by saying, "If I were you, I would or would not…" I always thought, *You are not me, so I am going to…*

Chantal Sutherland, who made history by being the first woman jockey to ride in the world's richest horse race, said, *"You have to stick it through and believe in yourself. You can't give up. So many times people told me I can't do this or can't do that. My nature is that I do not listen very well. I'm very determined, and I believe in myself. My parents brought me up that way. Thank God for that. I do not let anything stand in my way."*

Inside Stuff – Cleaning Your Junk Drawer

While surviving the chaos of our daily lives, we begin to treat our minds like junk drawers. Do you have that drawer in the kitchen filled with a boatload of miscellaneous items? Have you ever attempted to clean it out and found things you could never find in the past? Have you ever gone through a junk drawer looking for a pen or pencil, but all you could put your hands on was the screwdriver you were looking for last week?

Sometimes, our minds are like those junk drawers. We put things in there or allow others to put things in there that do not belong. We allow stuff to get dumped in a particular place in which it is not supposed to be. We are either too lazy or too forgetful to remember where those items go. Have you ever examined what is in a junk drawer? A mismatch of any and everything! A tangled, mangled mess, where nothing is distinguishable. Junk minds are like junk drawers and in the midst of them, you can always find frustration and a disturbance of peace because of the mess and disorganization.

"Today is the day to break free from the prison of the person you know yourself to be and step into a self you have yet to know. Will it be comfortable? No, but do it anyway."

Debbie Ford

What about an overcrowded dresser drawer? Socks and underwear, tops and bottoms all pushed and mashed into one overcrowded, undersized drawer! Trying to close it will take more time and energy than you bargained for! When it's closed, it looks all nice and neat, but what's really in there?

One of the advantages of being disorganized is the joy of discovery! - A.A. Milne
Clean up! You never know what treasure you may find!

We need to clean our junk drawers. Our minds need a good cleaning of all the junk we've allowed to be dumped there. It needs organizing and a clean sweep of all the debris accumulated there.

Thoughts that have plagued us need to be wiped away and saturated with a sanitizer. They usually came from words spoken to us or over us, but we allowed them to stay inside. We need to dispel the myths that have contaminated us with thoughts and conclusions based on erroneous information. It is interesting how cars, houses and buildings get cleaned and organized, and many other things get evaluated, but we seldom investigate why we think the way we do, and how we think about ourselves. Our thoughts, our perspectives and what we believe really form us. They make us who we are and the only way to change and grow is to change how we think.

So, how do you accomplish that change? You have to fight to clean the drawer! First, you must dump everything out and start over. You must organize everything that goes into the drawer and before allowing it to go back in, you must *evaluate* it all! Is there a better place for it? Is it needed at all? Does it belong with other things not in this drawer? Does it belong to me? Is it someone else's stuff? Little by little, the evaluation process eliminates the misplaced and the displaced, and over the course of time, the drawer will get cleaned and organized. The fight to keep a tidy drawer does not end, but it does become second nature in time. So it is with our minds, the first spring cleaning will be the hardest, but we must empty it of thoughts that do not line up with God's word and a positive self-image. And like cleaning the drawer, keeping our minds clean will become second nature.

The cost associated with clutter can be enormous. If clutter in the physical realm drains your energy and can affect your mood as well as your outlook on life, just imagine the clutter of confusing, negative thoughts in your mind. The effects are even more gargantuan. The mind needs decluttering. We need a receptionist at the entrance to the mind, and every thought that comes has to check in before being allowed to enter. They cannot be allowed to hide behind the pain of the past.

Everything must be exposed and emptied out so we can begin to view ourselves and the world as the masterpiece it truly is. The pain of the past serves no purpose for you, it is simply junk in your drawer. Give back what does not belong to you, discard what is useless. Keep only what is meaningful and beneficial. A well-organized drawer makes it so much easier to locate what you are looking for. The answers you are searching for exist within yourself; it helps to have a clear mind in order to clearly see.

How Do You Treat Yourself?

Do you willingly pay for everything for others? Do you give all that you have to please others all the while neglecting yourself? Do you treat yourself poorly, allowing others to reap everything you have to offer? You

"The way you treat yourself sets the standard for others."

Sonya Friedman

should neither over indulge yourself nor neglect yourself. Recognize your value and worth.

Many times, I have spoken with women who will do anything and buy anything to have the company of a man. I once had a married friend whose husband wanted to divorce her. She promised him easy chairs, big screen TV's, and new clothes. She said she would provide everything he wanted if he would just stay with her. How demeaning! Even though God hates divorce, He allows it because of the hardness of man's heart. He would not want a woman to belittle herself or resort to bribery or other means to keep a man. If a man does not want to be with a woman, nothing will make him stay long term. Gifts and other benefits may keep him temporarily, but a long-term, committed relationship is not possible if each person is not properly valued and honored.

I have met many young women who protested when I corrected them about taking care of their boyfriends. These were guys who would impregnate the ladies and then push them back to work before the baby was even a month old. Then, they thought it was robbery to even marry them. I have also met young women who worked every day and prospered. I witnessed them give away all they had financially, mentally and physically. Finally, they began to fall into ruin and suffering, but the guys still asked, or rather, demanded even more.

This mistreatment of oneself and accepting abuse to be inflicted on them is a product of low self-esteem and worth. Belief in self, plus having dreams and goals, are necessary to overcome the enemies of self. Too often who we are is undervalued, and what we have is overvalued.

Realistic views of self are necessary to assess where we are, but we can always change to be a better self if we are positive and do not lose hope. Zayn Malik said, *"Just because you do not have a prince, doesn't mean you're not a princess."* Also, when evaluating "inside stuff," we must learn and practice focus. I think about the Bible story of Nehemiah rebuilding the wall around Jerusalem after it had been destroyed. Many tried to get him to change his focus and fight a battle that he most assuredly could have won. But to move from his focus would have taken him away from his purpose.

We have to learn that not all battles are worth fighting. Battles of other people's opinions are not worthy opponents of your time.

The only worthwhile battle actually worth fighting is the one on the inside so that you are a better you.

The Virtual SPA Experience

How should you treat yourself? Very well, and with regard for the masterpiece you are. You should visit a SPA. It is worth the investment. For instance, I love, love, love going to the spa! Since I've become an adult, I treat myself occasionally to the spa…foot spas, day spas, hotels with spas, destination spas for massages, facials, manicures, pedicures, and body wraps. They are wonderful and can be medicinal. Any kind of spa treatment is marvelous and beneficial. But how do you treat yourself?

Webster defines spa as "a place where water that has many minerals in it comes up naturally from the ground and where people go to improve their health by swimming in, bathing in, or drinking the water." The spa dates back to ancient Roman times. It's a place where you can go for medicinal purposes…to get rejuvenated and healed. People submerge themselves in the mineral waters and drink of the healing waters to restore wholeness and health.

You should treat yourself to *SPA Treatment Thoughts* as well. Know that you are valuable, for a mental revitalization can be just as powerful as a visit to a physical spa. My first experience in the spa was wholly peaceful. I discovered tranquility and learned how to relax like I never had before. The power of meditation discovered there can be life changing. I remember, after spending some time there, getting into the car to head home thinking *I will not go back to my life,* and I really never went back. How do I capture that moment without spending hundreds of dollars on a spa treatment? I had to reinvent the thoughts and feelings of going to a spa by focusing on who God says I am.

I cannot always go to the physical spa, so when I need some healing, when I need to drink the mineral water, when clarity is needed and my health is in need of attention, I visit the Virtual Spa to regain balance and find healing.

These are some of the *SPA Treatment Thoughts* that I focus on when I am not able to visit the physical spa:

Who You Are

Special Powerful Awesome!
Sensible Peculiar Amenable
Spiritually sound, Passionate Actionable
Support Possibilities Achieve
Still Plainly Alive!
Sealed Protected Appointed
Significant Purposeful Accepted
Super Prosperous Alliance
Strong Patient Able
Someone Pleasant and Approachable
Sustainable Prolific Amazing

What God Has Done

Spirit Poured Again and again for you
Spoken Powerful Affirmations
Sanctified Purified Amplified
Spread His Peace Abroad
Saved Positioned Anointed

What You Should Do

Seek Peace Always
Speak positively. Pay yourself in savings and rest. Allow yourself to make mistakes
Synchronize, Pamper and Absorb yourself in the goodness of God!
Separate and sanctify yourself. Position yourself on the Altar
Surrender Personally All to God. Visit the SPA often
Sincere Pleasing Assured
Stop Pretending Always
Settle Personal Affairs
Sense Pray Acknowledge
Sin + Pain = Avoid
See Pave Push Ahead
Submit Prepare Act
Slow Pierced Anger
Seeking Peering Admitting
Sow Prosper Abide
Surround Press Abound
Secret Place Abide (Psalm 91)
Sovereign Presence Acknowledged
Source is God. Performance for God. Approval from God alone
Security in God. Purpose in God. Acceptance by God
Scripture Plans Acknowledge
SHALL PRAISE ALWAYS!!!

GIVE YOURSELF SOME SPA TREATMENTS DAILY!!!

Invest in Yourself

We must invest in ourselves with the help of the Holy Ghost so that we can have healthy relationships with others. We need the help of the Holy Ghost in our marriage, business, workplace, marketplace, in our homes with our children, with our parents and particularly those in the body of Christ. However, take note: if you do not know who you are, and you do not like who you are, you really cannot expect somebody else to like you either. Take *SPA Treatment* moments to reassess thoughts, refocus and refresh. You are worth the time and the effort.

"Today you are you, that is truer than true. There is no one alive who is Youer than You."

Dr. Seuss, Happy Birthday to You!

Invest in yourself. It is the greatest investment, even in the financial realm. Ben Franklin said, *"For the best return on your money, pour your purse into your head."* God designed you to have an impact for the blessing of others and for the glory of His kingdom. Sometimes, that also means you must spend resources on yourself to receive special training or learn more about how to communicate with others. Learn to appreciate the unique contributions you can make to the lives of others who are hurting and rejected.

My college professor, J.E.B. Shy in Marketing 101 always said, *"The*

human investment is the best investment." Invest in other people and help them win so that you can win. Invest in books that encourage and challenge you, take classes and go to seminars that enhance you and teach you how to win with people. Never underestimate the value of corporate worship services and the fellowship of the believers. Leaders at my church say that your presence makes a difference and your absence makes a difference. Because you are valuable and others are too, together you are a force to be reckoned with, so do not neglect assembling with forward moving and thinking people of God.

You must have a good self-image and have your focus in the right place to have right relationships with others. I'm not talking about being self-consumed, arrogant, or self-centered. Instead, we must really focus on the things of God, His kingdom, and getting all the attention off ourselves. Truthfully, it is very selfish to think bad about yourself. It is really false humility. It is self-serving, and it does not honor God. Begin assessing your thoughts. If you can get a new thought, you can change your life.

A transforming life can be achieved by obeying Romans 12:1-2 that reads, *"I beseech you therefore, brethren, by the mercies of God, that ye present your bodies a living sacrifice, holy, acceptable unto God, which is your reasonable service. And be not conformed to this world: but be ye transformed by the renewing of your mind, that ye may prove what is that good, and acceptable, and perfect, will of God."* John Maxwell has stated that if you change your thinking first, then you change your behavior. It is time to decide to love yourself. Be confident in the decisions you make. Learn to laugh at yourself. Now, forget that which is behind and press toward the goal. When you make a mistake – and you will because we're all human – forgive yourself and repent. It is so useless to walk around feeling guilty. It robs us, and it only exists to cause us to fail. So, forgive yourself and move on.

Philippians 4:8 says, "Finally, brethren, whatsoever things are true, whatsoever things are honest, whatsoever things are just, whatsoever things are pure, whatsoever things are lovely, whatsoever things are good report; if there be any virtue, and if there be any praise, think on these things."

Do not allow yourself to be stranded in the mud of a world gone wrong. God is at work in you. *Philippians 3:13-14 says, "Brethren, I count not myself to have apprehended: but this one thing I do, forgetting those things which are behind, and reaching forth unto those things which are before, I press towards the mark for the*

prize of the high calling of God in Christ Jesus." I press toward the goal to win the supreme and heavenly prize to which God and Christ Jesus is calling us upward. Therefore, do not compare yourself to or compete with others.

A lot of people who know me say, *"Oh you're so competitive."* Perhaps, but I do not compete with people. I compete with myself. Proverbs says iron sharpens iron, and I use other people to sharpen myself. I look at who I am and where I am (See Proverbs 27:17). I ask God, *"What else is it that you want me to do?"* I want to compete against myself so that I can go higher…I can be better in God. It's not about competition with anyone else, but it is about competition in making myself better.

I have invested in myself over the years by first spending time with God,

attending seminars, listening endlessly to recorded teachings, reading books and journaling. I spent a great deal of time listening to recordings of teachings from the Word of God. I remember dubbing cassette tapes from friends so I could get the Word of God in my hands and get it into my spirit. I would use travel time to put in a cassette in the car and listen on the way to work, on the way home, and to the grocery store. Whenever and whatever time I could devote, I spent ingesting the Scriptures.

I would cry before the Lord asking Him to change me and grow me. I was so hungry for the Word and for change. I knew it was the only thing that could help me by the power of the Holy Spirit. You see, I couldn't afford professional help. My counselor was the Holy Spirit. If I could have paid for a professional counselor, I would have gone. The stigma of being labeled as "crazy" did not bother me because I was desperate to be free.

I thought for a time the television minister, Joyce Meyer, was reading my mail, but it was the Holy Spirit using her to speak to me and to the issues with which I was dealing. I knew other people were not to blame for the sadness I often experienced. I was looking for answers. The devil kept trying to sell me his solutions, but I knew they were both temporary and false. The only real, permanent answers would come from God Himself. I thank God for His Son, in the person of Jesus Christ and the power of the Holy Spirit to help me grow, change and develop.

It was then and is (now) so important to me to be in right relationship with others and I knew I had to be right on the inside for that to be a reality for me. I also learned the power of declaring a thing and the power of a decision. I had to change my mind, decide to be different, and daily declare I was different! The journey has not been easy; it has been an uphill battle, but transformation has occurred. Change is still happening as I continue to yield to God.

Apply Your Gifts to Bless the Lives of Others

You have been given a unique combination of spiritual gifts, natural abilities and experiences that can potentially create great value for others. If you refuse to accept the truth about how God wants your life to enrich others, you will focus on your own real and imagined limitations. You will resist entering new relationships and will restrain yourself from opening up to those closest to you. The consequences can scar the lives of your children, your spouse, other family, your friends and work associates – ultimately, the world is diminished because you imagined you had nothing worth offering. Are you are still believing those lies that cause you to look at yourself through the blind eyes of men or are you seeing yourself to be the person God says you are?

YOUR THOUGHTS AND SELF SPEECH REFLECTION

Voices in Your Inner Circle

Due to a lifelong struggle to clean up my private life, I am very protective of who I allow into my inner circle. I often take time to contemplate. Who am I around? Who surrounds me? I want to make sure old habits and patterns do not recur.

It is necessary to learn how to combat all things negative in order to realize the true happiness you seek. Really not so much as achieving happiness, but more to find joy; happiness is contingent on circumstances, joy, on the other hand, comes from the inside. Joy is not emotional; rather, it is a decision that we choose to make.

"A year or so ago, I went through all the people in my life and I asked myself: does this person inspire me, genuinely love me and support me unconditionally? I wanted nothing but positive influences in my life."

Mena Suvari

Those you allow to influence you can impact you, either in a positive or negative way. If the voices speaking to you from the outside do not agree with your inner voices, then you should have those voices evaluated. This is not to suggest that you find a personal cheerleader;

Opinions are like noses, everybody has one and they usually have holes in them.

instead, you need to find individuals who will encourage you to be a better person, to grow, and to change.

If the voices add value to you, inspiring you to add value to others, then listen to those voices. I am also not advocating "yes men," but those who will hold you accountable without judgment. You need people who encourage and promote, and do not degrade…those who will do more than just tolerate you, but also celebrate you. You should only allow voices that lift and stretch you as a person, not those that distract and downgrade.

We need to, on a regular basis, evaluate the people we have in our lives.

If they are not lifting us up or challenging us to be better, then it is not to say that they are bad people, but perhaps you have outgrown them and it is now time to engage a new sphere of influence. Some people are just temporary in your life, only there for a sole purpose. Although they may still be in your life, their influence on your decisions and who you choose to be should remain limited.

Not every individual with whom you come into contact should be allowed to influence your thinking and thus your actions. You should, however, be very selective about who you choose as your advisors and counselors, who you listen to for guidance.

Inner circles should be small and the voices they use should be big, loud, and full of wisdom. I often compartmentalize my friends and associates. I realized a long time ago that some people were only good for distinctively particular things in my life, while others were good for other things. There were also those people who were toxic and should not be in my life at all. That's all part of the evaluation process. Additionally, some people fade away over time because of our ever changing lives. If we are ever growing, changing, and continually adjusting our attitudes, then our very selves will consequently be changing, adjusting and growing. Therefore, it would no longer be advantageous to flow in the same circles we once had.

We will never be where we are needed if we never let go and release those people and situations in our lives that keep us among the "just okay" and hold back the real greatness in us.

We know that in order for a flower to blossom, it must have the right soil and the right seed. That being said, in order for you to reach your full potential, you have to be in an environment that nurtures growth. People we select to be a part of our inner circle must be individuals who nurture our potential. Those individuals that try to confine you to a certain level of living are hazardous to your dreams and should not be allowed to remain anywhere around you. A confining environment will only stunt your growth. Although you can use the hazardous material as fuel for your engine, you cannot run on that fuel long term.

People in your inner circle can energize you to be all you have been called to be and do. They can cheer you on and help you do the same for others. They also challenge you when you need it, and they celebrate with you in your success.

John Maxwell said, "What we say to ourselves either encourages us or discourages us. The words we need to embrace are positive words such as we, can, will and yes. What do we need to eliminate? Me, can't, won't and no."

Pay Attention to What You Are Thinking

Let's look at what God has to say about who we are, which enables us to have a healthy relationship with ourselves. First, we have to accept that God made us and whatever God made is good. *"So God created man in his own image, in the image of God created He him; male and female created He them"* (Genesis 1:27).

Also, the Bible says, *"For we are his workmanship, created in Christ Jesus unto good works, which God hath before ordained that we should walk in them"*(Ephesians 2:10). So, build yourself up in the Holy Ghost, agree with God and listen to what God has to say about you and not that which other people have to say about you. Pay attention to your thinking because this is the true battle ground. This is where the devil tries to beat us up.

The fight to stay free from bad thinking is a daily struggle. I cannot emphasize more, the need for us to transform the thoughts we have allowed to live in our minds (See Romans 12:1-2).

We also need to be cautious of how we speak to children. We are molding and shaping them for the future. My mother used to say some negative things about me, but over time, God has done such a miraculous work on me that I cannot remember most of what she said.

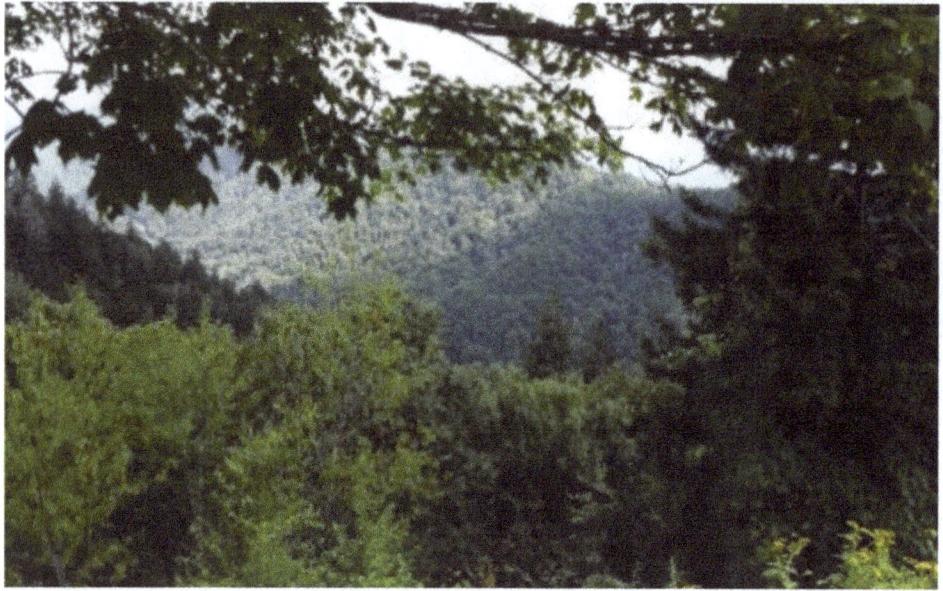

We need to shift attention from whatever anybody says about us that is constantly disturbing our minds and personalities. These are not God's thoughts about us. Always keep your mind focused on Him. It's not about your trying to create a better version of yourself; rather, it is focusing on God and being all He has called you to be.

Change the Voice in Your Head

The words expressed inwardly about yourself, put there by your own thought patterns or those allowed to be planted by someone else, must be transformed so that you walk as a "happy self." Saying things like, "Nobody likes me...Poor me...I'm not good enough...I'm too fat...I'm too skinny...I do not try hard enough...I do not deserve it...I'm just waiting for the other shoe to drop," are all focused on you in a negative way, and that is a wrong focus.

Remember, *"Death and life are in the power of the tongue: and they that love it shall eat the fruit thereof"* (Proverbs 18:21). Do you know who you believe more than anyone else? Yourself. So, if you are filling your head with a slew of negativity, you will have a difficult time attaining the 'you' that God has called you to be. You cannot believe or allow wrong thought patterns to enter and stay in your mind.

We need to change the voice that is in our heads, and we need to begin to agree with the voice of God. The practice of speaking God's word over your life daily is a good habit to form.

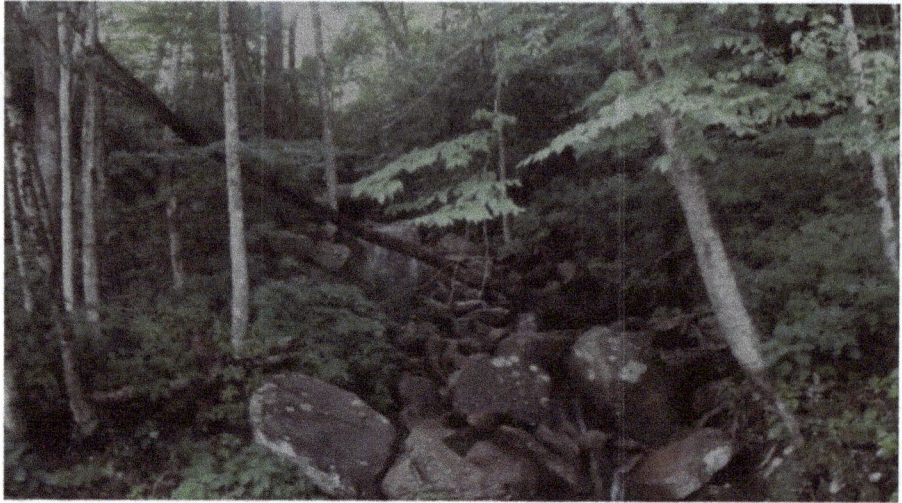

INNER CONFLICT RESOLUTION...

- Be aware there is a problem – forget the past
- Control emotions and behavior
- Be attentive to your thoughts – take time for meditation and reflection
- Work towards resolutions – seek ways to move in a positive direction
- Follow your passion
- Do not fear change

Apostle Paul wrote, *"For whether we live, we live unto the Lord and whether we die, we die unto the Lord: whether we live therefore, or, die, we are the Lord's"* (Romans 14:8).

Therefore, if Christ came that we may live an abundant life, we should then strive to make sure that our lives and thoughts are in agreement with God. We need to make an active effort to change our thinking perspectives and to grasp that life. It begins with a decision to be different. We cannot be different unless our thoughts are different. And very often they need to be radically different. Your thoughts should go through a radical adjustment and should always be purposeful.

Loving and Valuing Yourself

When you love yourself, you are at peace. Find peace with the one who made you and peace will be contained within you. When you do not value yourself, you are allowing people to steal your peace. At the root of being at peace with yourself and others is forgiveness, that is to choose not to hold someone hostage for a committed wrong.

Peace is characterized by the lack of conflict-inclined behaviors and freedom from fear of violence. It is also commonly understood as the absence of hostility and retribution; peace also suggests sincere attempts at reconciliation, and the existence of healthy or newly healed interpersonal or international relationships. In addition, peace advocates prosperity in matters of social or economic welfare.

In a blog post, Joel Osteen said that some people can be peace stealers and we should walk away from them.[1] He indicated in his research that he read a study, which stated that for every happy friend you have, you are twenty percent more likely to be happy most of the time. Technically, you

"Happiness, true happiness, is an inner quality. It is a state of mind. If your mind is at peace, you are happy. If your mind is at peace, but you have nothing else, you can be happy. If you have everything the world can give - pleasure, possessions, power - but lack peace of mind, you can never be happy."

Dada Vaswani

---

[1] Osteen, Joel. "Walk Away from Peace Stealers." Joel and Victoria's Blog. May 20, 2016. www.Joelosteen.com.

can interpret that to mean if you can just find five happy friends, there's a good chance you're going to be happy. This is what the scripture says, *"He that walketh with wise men shall be wise..."*(Proverbs 13:20). This is also true in the negative, just like in the positive.

Think of it this way, for every peace stealer you allow into your life, you are twenty percent more likely to live stressed, on edge, or have a crisis. Why wouldn't you want to focus on finding happy friends? I agree with Joel that many people are stuck because of who they have in their lives. If you love and value yourself, you will be very selective about those you allow into your life.

SPA Treatment Moment
Evaluate your acquaintances. Are they Sincere, Piquant and Actual? Are they Super, Prosperous Alliances or do they weigh and drag you down?

Additionally, if you love and value yourself, you will take time to practice self-care. I said this before and it bears mentioning again, evaluate the people you allow into your life. You have to ask who's in your life, and to whom and what types of relationships do you give attention, energy and time? Are you the 'rescue ranger' always running to the aid of someone in crisis? Are you always trying to please others to your own detriment? Are you just worn out and overwhelmed trying to take care of everyone else but yourself? You will never please everybody all of the time, so why try?

We are intricate beings, full of gifts and grace. Precious jewels and treasures that are uniquely our own, reside within each and every human being. However, if you do not value yourself, it is equivalent to climbing to the top of Mt. Everest with millions in diamonds and throwing them off the top of the mountain. Very valuable precious stones of no use to anyone because care was not taken with them. They will be scattered everywhere and be of little use until they are discovered, shined and held in high regard.

Take a look in the mirror, and decide to say, "You are useful, important, worthwhile, and intrinsically valuable." Remember that you belong to God!

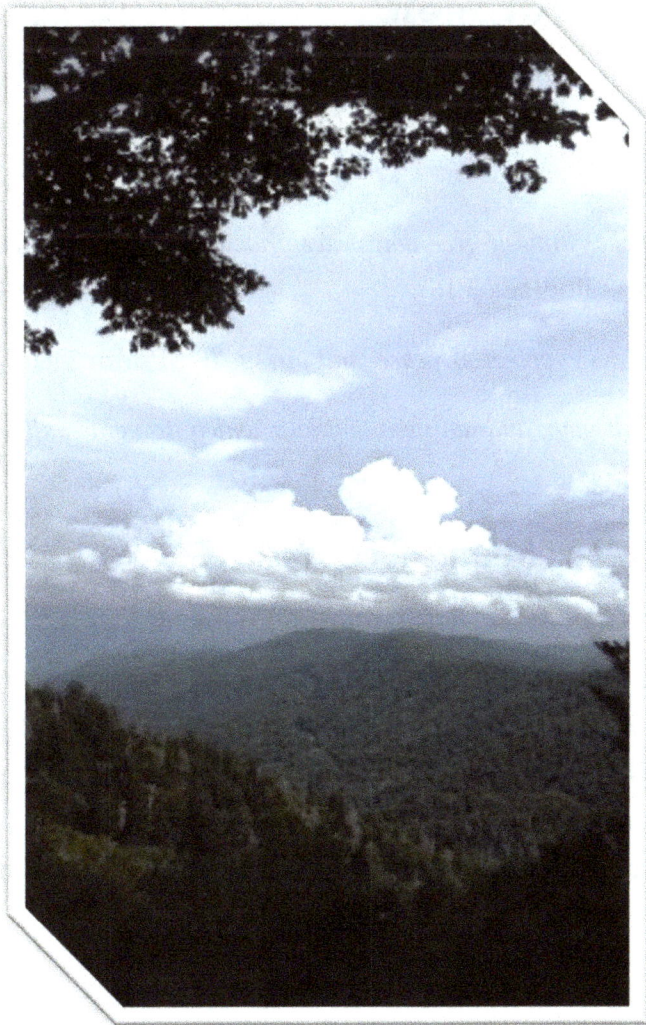

Value yourself enough to reassess, refocus and reevaluate your need for friends who will add value to your life as you bring value to theirs.

Be at Peace with Yourself

Decide today to pursue peace, love yourself and also pay attention to what you say. Furthermore, it is important to know what God's Word says about peace.

"Now the Lord of peace himself give you peace always by all means. The Lord be with you all" (2 Thessalonians 3:16).

"Depart from evil and do good; seek peace, and pursue it" (Psalm 34:14).

"Follow peace with all men, and holiness, without which no man shall see the Lord" (Hebrew 12:14).

Once you have been accepted by God, He separates you for His purpose. Since each one of us has been declared holy in our behavior and devout with Godly qualities, we ought to be a person consecrated with holy behavior and devout in Godly qualities (See 2 Peter 3:11-14). This is why we all are waiting and earnestly longing for the day of the coming of the Lord. While focusing on yourself in a negative way, you cannot be what God has called you to be. You cannot be at peace.

Constantly dwelling on your past failures, negatives or pain is a sure way to remain stuck and locked in an unfavorable position. Replaying and reliving the hurts of past offenses produces torment, not peace. No peace can be obtained by entertaining encore performances of past assaults.

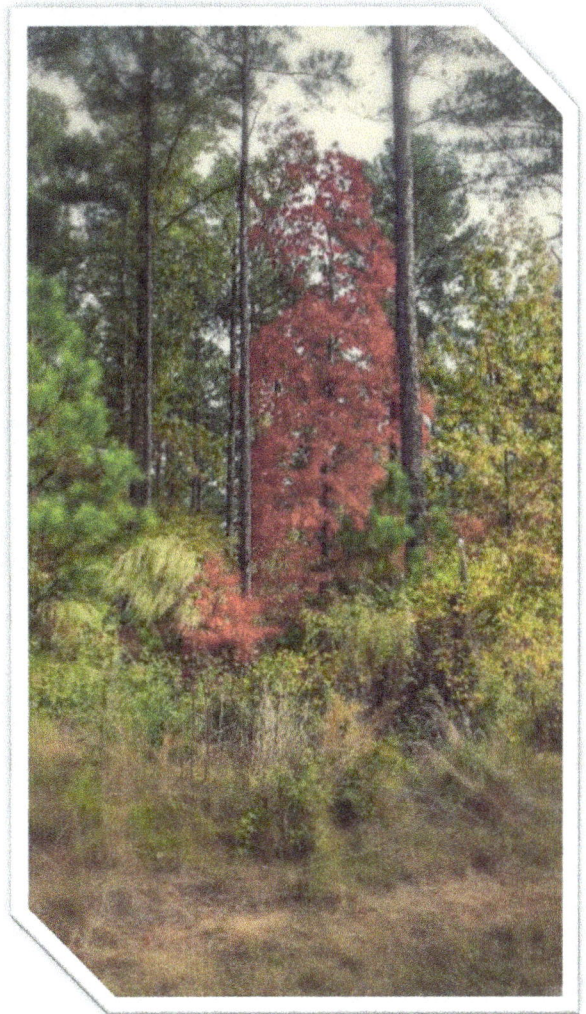

You cannot be a holy, consecrated person with Godly qualities simply because you are too focused on the wrong things. Decide to enter into the peace of God so that you may find peace within yourself.

SPA Treatment Moment

Decide to let go of the past, decide to forgive, and decide to have peace.

Seal. Promise. Avow

Value Yourself to Achieve Your Dreams

Who you are, including your dreams, will not be more important to someone else as it is to you. Yes, you are the only one who will have a vested interest in your life and in your dreams. Many times, we want others to value us, we want them to consider us important to their lives and we want them to take an interest in our dreams. However, not every one is going to be that for you and not everyone will care about you or your dreams. Therefore, it is up to you to value yourself and know who you are, thus ending the need for others to know you and to see you as important.

Your emotional and mental health is very important and you cannot risk damaging your health by means of always trying to rescue others. It is important that you realize that you are not going to be able to help everyone, not even the ones you love. If they do not want the help or resent the fact that it is coming from you, then there is nothing you can do for them, except to keep praying.

I have heard it said, in your twenties you wonder what people are saying about you, in your forties you do not care what people are saying about you, and in your sixties you realize nobody was thinking about you.

Moreover, do not allow those who do not value you to prevent you from reaching out and being there for those who do truly need and value what you have to offer. But make sure you are helping others because you want to help them and not because you are looking for them to value or validate you.

Value yourself first and strengthen your core self. Only then will you become emotionally healthy and strong for others.

"Life is too short to waste any amount of time on wondering what other people think about you. In the first place, if they had better things going on in their lives, they wouldn't have the time to sit around and talk about you. The important thing to me is not others' opinions of me, but my opinion of myself."

C. Joy Bell

Ask yourself if you are living your life to its full potential. Know that every aspect of your life should be used for a purpose and that fulfilling that purpose would complete your being. When you know how to use your abilities for the common good, then you would feel better about others and about yourself. Therefore, you can learn to love and value yourself better.

When you know how to include other people in your joys, then you will go on to become a better person.

In addition, you should be guided by your dreams. You would have a better run at life if you know precisely what you want to achieve. Whether your goal is to conquer the world or just live a simple and happy life, it is always good to set a forthright direction to your life. This however does not necessarily mean that you cannot do impulsive things that would take you to different paths. In fact, impulsiveness may let you discover different things about yourself that you never would have known if not for those experiences. Just learn how to balance situations in your life and you would surely love and value yourself better.

SPA Treatment Moment

Learn to value yourself and be Spontaneous, Pleasant and have a great Attitude.

Do you think that you do not love and value yourself enough? Do you want to do things for yourself just this once? Then let go for a while and learn how to take time for yourself. You could never be content with your life if you do not love and value yourself enough.

How Do You Allow Others to Treat You?

"Believe people the first time that they show you who they are."- Maya Angelou

More often now we hear a lot of people speak about how important it is to teach people how to treat us. But what does this really mean? What does it actually entail? You either teach people to treat you with dignity and respect, or you don't. This means you are partly responsible for the mistreatment that you receive at the hands of someone else. You shape others' behavior when you teach them what they can get away with and what they cannot.

If you find yourself unhappy with how you are being treated, if you feel you are always being taken for granted, used, misused, or even abused by some of the people in your life, it is time you did a self-check. If the people in your life treat you in an undesirable manner, figure out what you are doing to reinforce, elicit, or allow that treatment.

Consider what happens if you are standing on the side of a cliff or if you are in a hole or a cave. If you make a sound, that sound will echo back whatever sound is made. Therefore, if you yell out 'help' it will reverberate help! If you say, with a loud voice, "You are stupid, bad and ugly," it will echo the same. Those comments will not be helpful to you, especially if you are stuck, but they will come back to you in the same manner that you put them out.

So, what happens if you call out that you are great or you need help or you are able. The sound will come back as positive and if you are stuck and you call for help, it will summon someone to your aid. What you send out, the vibes you emit, the messages you transmit, will be what you in-turn, attract. We do not attract what we want, we attract what we send out. Like an echo reverberating sounds in the atmosphere, what you put out is what you will receive. It will give others the signal on how to treat you!

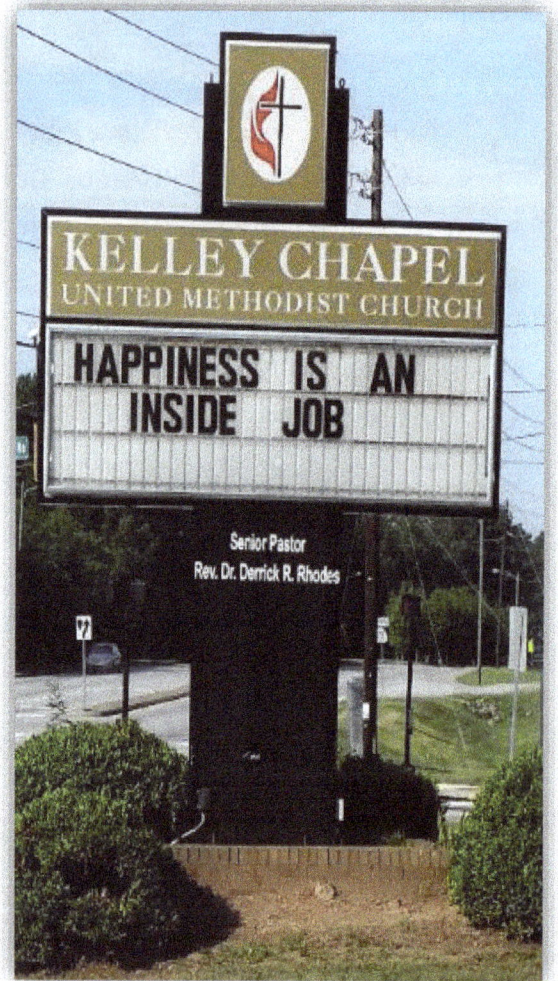

Identify the pay offs you may be giving someone in response to any negative behavior. For example, when people are aggressive, bossy or controlling and then get their way, you have rewarded them for their unacceptable behavior.

Because you are accountable, you can declare the relationship "reopened for negotiation" at any time you choose, and for as long as you choose. Even a relating pattern that is over 30 years old can be redefined. Before you reopen the negotiation, you must commit or do so from a position of strength and power, not fear and self-doubt. The resolve to be treated with dignity and respect must be without any compromise.

The worst thing you could do is make a lot of noise about changing things, only to revert to the old, familiar, and destructive patterns. To talk about change and not make the change is teaching others to treat your statements and declarations lightly. Where your relationship standards are concerned, commit to yourself that, although it may be difficult to affect change, you must not compromise. To compromise in this area is to sell out your most precious commodity; you.

There comes a pivotal time in our adult life that we have to say *no* to the lie that we are a victim. We are in our most vulnerable state when we feel like we have no control, because it is then that we actually allow ourselves to be controlled by others. When we surrender to the negative actions, decisions, and behaviors of others, we let them take the reins of our lives and lead us wherever they please.

Being healthy individuals means that we realize that we have some God-given abilities to control our lives, decisions, and even our relationships. We cannot control the behaviors of others, but we can always control how we respond to those behaviors, how we interpret those behaviors, and how we allow those behaviors to impact our lives.

RELATIONSHIP TO THE GREAT
INFINITE POWER

Have you ever been to a fair or circus where there was a house of mirrors? Every mirror is warped, reflecting a false, distorted image of the person in front of it. Similarly, many people have a false self-image because they look to other people to realize who they are. Unsuspectingly, those incorrect or warped perspectives have a profound impact on what they believe and feel about themselves as individuals.

"I had struggled so hard and so long that I simply exhausted myself, only to find that God had all the time in the world to wait for me to allow Him to free me."

Michelle McKinney Hammond

Sometimes, people can be cruel and send messages, which quickly and radically distort another person's idea of who they are. They may think they are worthless only because someone said so. They may believe that they are stupid because the most popular kid in class said so. They may even believe that they are ugly because one spiritually-blinded person could not see their real beauty. They may come to believe that there is no hope for someone like them, so why even try to make life any better?

After exposure to such perverse ideas about ourselves, we look into our bathroom mirrors and see flaws and features that we would otherwise change if we could. A girl suffering from anorexia who has already lost half her body weight would look into the mirror and still believe she is fat. The man who has the handsome features of a movie star can focus his attention so that he only sees that he has a big nose.

At school, a young man who started life with undiagnosed dyslexia or attention-deficit, can form a permanent picture of himself as too dumb to learn anything. A young lady with one rejection letter from a prestigious college, with far too many applicants, can imagine that she isn't good enough to succeed in a competitive world. Do you see the point? All of these people are looking into a warped mirror, reflecting false images about themselves instead of looking into the perfect mirror of God's Word.

> *True humility is not thinking less of yourself; it is thinking of yourself less. – C. S. Lewis.*

Knowing Your Worth to God

The Word of God says we are *"fearfully and wonderfully made"* (See Psalm 139:14). As humans, God originally created us to have great value and self-worth. We fail to appreciate this about ourselves if we do not agree with the Creator of the universe! I know who I am in God, and you also have to know who you are in God. Knowing who you are in God means that you can hardly be deterred or discouraged. I am not trying to convince you that I have arrived; rather, I am a work in progress. God loves us. He is rich in mercy. He has crowned us with His glory and honor.

"*Are not five sparrows sold for two farthings, and not one of them is forgotten before God? But even the very hairs of your head are all numbered. Fear not therefore: ye are of more value than many sparrows*" (Luke 12:6-7). The Bible says that if God were to punish everyone for their sins, no one would be alive. (See Psalm 130:3). Jesus took our place so that we would not experience the suffering and pain of death. His love is astounding! His actions are palpable evidence that we are indeed of value to Him.

In the Bible, Jesus tells us to love God above all things, and then to love our neighbors as ourselves. "*And to love Him with all the heart, and with all the understanding, and with all the soul, and with all the strength, and to love his neighbor as himself, is more than all whole burnt offerings and sacrifices*" (Mark 12:33).

If you do not like yourself, loving your neighbor would prove to be a particularly difficult task. This is the most likely reason for the high rates of crime and hate in the world. "*For as much as ye know that ye were not redeemed with corruptible things, as silver and gold, from your vain conversation received by tradition from your fathers; But with the precious blood of Christ, as of a lamb without blemish and without spot."* (1 Peter 1:18-19)

What Does God Think and Say about You?

God knows you better than you know yourself. He knows the number of hairs on your head. Whether you purchased yours and whether you have fuzz on top or grew it naturally. God knows the number of hairs of head – this demonstrates how much He knows and cares about us. (See Matthew 10:30). He knows you, and He has great plans for you. *"For I know the plans and thoughts that I have for you,' says the Lord, 'plans for peace and well-being and not for disaster to give you a future and a hope."* (Jeremiah 29:11). He describes it as an "expected end!" None of this is unplanned. God is purposeful, and He has planned for you to prosper and be in good health even as your soul prospers (See 1 Peter 1:18-19).

You are the apple of God's eye. He declares that when He made you it was good! God says, *"I am the Creator, and you are my creation. I breathed into your nostrils the breath of life"* (Genesis 2:7).

"I created you in my own image" (Genesis 1:27).

"My eyes saw your unformed substance before you were born" (Psalm 139:16).

"For You did form my inward parts; You did knit me together in my mother's womb. I will give thanks and praise to You, for I am fearfully and wonderfully made" (Psalm 139:13-14).

God has great plans for you.

God declares that you are valuable! He said, *"I have crowned you with glory and honor as the pinnacle and final act of the six days of creation"* (Psalm 8:5, Genesis 1:26). He sent His own Son to show you how to live on this earth, who then gave His life for you. God says that you are His, and nothing can snatch you out of His hands.

"Man looks on the outward appearance, but God looks on the heart" (1 Samuel 16:7). This statement is absolutely true. However, the person who knows God loves and cherishes him or her, will have a face radiating with inner confidence, peace, and joy that can perceptibly have an effect on other expressions. This can then translate into smiles rather than tense squinting or angry frowns.

Knowing that God loves and cherishes you can transform the outer appearance as well. Unfortunately, many people walk around with expressions spawned by all the impertinent ideas they have absorbed from people about themselves.

You Were Designed by God

Think for a moment about a golf ball, which is purposefully designed to help it go further faster. The dimple reduces drag and maximizes carry. The core is engineered for extreme speed and outstanding feel. Like the golf ball, we are designed by the great Creator to reduce drag, in order that we may be thrust in the direction of our destiny. Our capacity to carry the assignment is maximized by His grace and mercy.

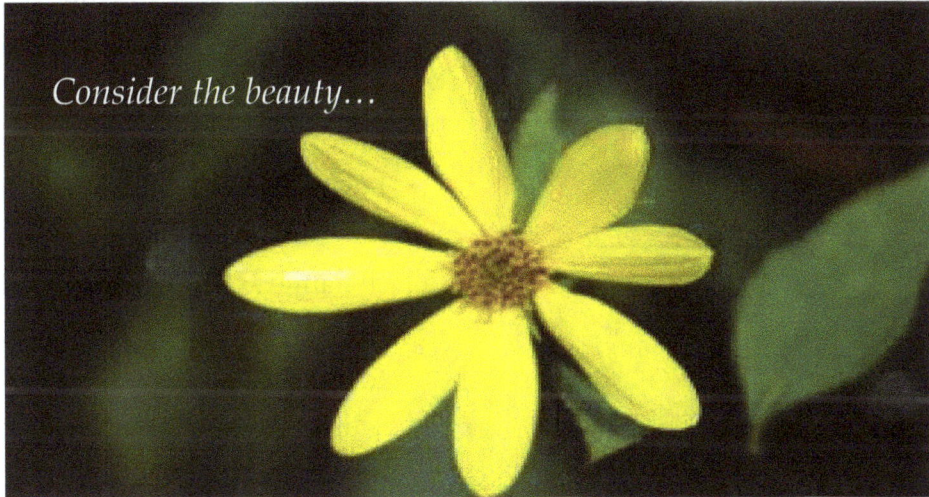

Consider the beauty…

We are engineered in His image, to move by His spirit, and to show the world His glory.

Establishing a Powerful Relationship with God

Through prayer, reading the Word of God, and making Him a priority in your life, you can establish an essential relationship with Him. However, you must first have a relationship with His Son, Jesus Christ.

Our God is an awesome God!

Once that connection is established, you surely then are on your way to Him. With the Holy Spirit living within you, you are on your way to a victorious life. Victorious, however, not problem free!

We can establish a dynamic relationship with God by keeping our minds focused on Him. There is so much argument because the enemy has blinded the minds of all sinners, and sometimes, even saints. He has persuaded some of us to take our minds off the true and living God. He has tried to fill our minds with all kinds of lies to keep our minds solely on ourselves. Do not allow the enemy to cause you to elevate yourself to

God's level through your own power, instead of recognizing and submitting yourself to God. Focusing on yourself too much is not God's plan. In addition, when you are negative, when you have low self-esteem, or when you do not say good things about yourself, you're in disagreement with God. *"Thou wilt keep him in peace, whose mind is stayed on thee: because he trusteth in thee"* (Isaiah 26:3).

Relationships are like a bank account. The more positive things you deposit, the more it grows.

When a withdrawal is necessary, there is something to draw from. This is somewhat similar to the concept of taking withdrawals from your bank account. If you're routinely withdrawing money from your account without making any deposits, you will eventually bring your account to zero and may even cause it show a negative balance, with no further resources to draw from.

We establish a powerful relationship with God by confessing what the Word says about us. Relationships are an investment. The more you put in, the more you can get back. With that said, you should invest in a relationship with yourself by confessing what God says about you. Romans 3:22 says we are the *"righteousness of God."* I heard a minister say, "Jesus never said I have. He always said I am." When you say, "I have," that means something was given to you. You can lose it because it can be taken away. Because the Holy Ghost is living inside of me, I can say with all confidence, "I am the righteousness of God." God's favor is not on me, but in me, Hallelujah! It is in me. Get in agreement with God.

Jesus declares, *"Ye are the light of the world. A city that is set on a hill cannot be hidden"* (Matthew 5:14). Personalize that statement by saying, "I am the light of the world."

"But ye are a chosen generation, a royal priesthood, a holy nation, a peculiar people; that ye should shew forth the praises of him who hath called you out of darkness into his marvelous light" (1 Peter 2:9). Confess that truth in your own life by saying, "I am part of a chosen generation, a royal priesthood, a holy nation, a peculiar (meaning extraordinary) people."

Blessed shalt thou be in the city, and blessed shalt thou be in the field. Blessed shall be the fruit of thy body, and the fruit of thy ground, and the fruit of thy cattle, the increase of thy kine, and the flocks of thy sheep" (Deuteronomy 28:3-4). I am blessed wherever I am and with whatever I am doing.

"Keep me as the apple of the eye, hide me under the shadow of thy wings" (Proverbs 17:8). Because of God's Word, we can declare that we are the apple of God's eye. When He looks in His hand and He sees me, He sees the apple of His eye.

"I will praise thee; for I am fearfully and wonderfully made: marvelous are thy works; and that my soul knoweth right well" **(Psalms 139:14). We can say that we are fearfully and wonderfully made. Have you praised God for how He made you?** Many people complain about some of their physical features, not understanding that every one of our characteristics has a glorious purpose. Even those who have some limitations can misunderstand. They may even believe it is a kind of divine punishment for some unknown offense. Instead, even our limitations are part of how God created us. They are part of our uniqueness, and they enable us to accomplish things someone lacking that physical feature would not be able to do.

Take the baseball, which is uncomplicated in appearance. At face value, it is a precision-made object that has often been the subject of controversy throughout its history. During this century, baseballs have not changed a lot, physically in size or in the materials used. However, some have contested that the balls have secretly been "pumped up" to increase the output of homeruns, to make the game more exciting. The manufacturers of baseballs and Major League Baseball have denied such allegations.

Unlike the baseball, the human being can be very complicated in appearance. But just like the baseball, man is made with precision. Formed from the dust of the earth, we have the breath of God flowing through us. We do not, however, deny that a born again believer can be "pumped up," and filled with the Holy Spirit to increase our output, and our effectiveness to make life more exciting.

When His super is put on our natural, we have the ability to be miraculous beings here on earth! The Word declares that we can do all things through Christ, who strengthens us (See Philippians 4:13). In our relationship with God, He gives us the ability to do the amazing!

Although our design is majestic and perfect, we still have flaws and imperfections within each of us. But that does not stop God from using us. As we cultivate a relationship with God, He deals with us concerning the internal affairs of our heart. He builds character in us and allows us to grow through the very many trials and tribulations in life. He teaches us to love, to forgive, to be forgiven when we trust everything to Him.

"For you formed my inward parts; you knitted me together in my mother's womb" (Psalm 139:13). Just like the dimples previously mentioned with golf balls, you were designed that way purposefully so that you could go further. In the same way, our imperfections catapult us further because of our design. God uses imperfect beings made perfect by the blood of Jesus.

Essayist and philosopher Ralph Waldo Emerson wrote, "What lies behind us and what lies before us are tiny matters compared to what lies within us." Do you believe that? Our past is resolved through God's forgiveness of our sins. Our future is secure because of God's promises of the blessed hope of Christ's return. We can be confident of these, however, only because we have the Spirit of Christ within us.

Humorist and author Mark Twain said, "A man cannot be comfortable without his own approval." You are the center of every relationship. If you have the Holy Ghost in you, He will go with you, thus allowing you to be all God has ordained you to be. *"But how can any of us approve of ourselves if we have no confidence that we are accepted by God?"* (Ephesians 1:6).

He will bring it to pass because you have a purpose, a destiny inside of you. *"Our relationship with Him, built upon His love for us, is where everything begins"* (1 John 4:19). Being a better you, because you know and believe you are who God says you are, causes you to have better relationships.

4

RELATING AND CONNECTING TO OTHER PEOPLE

The Importance of Proper Relationships

Once your inner thoughts are on the right path, you will be able to form healthy relationships with others. Nothing is more important than the inner life.

I always hated to see others get exploited or mistreated. I know I would never allow someone to misuse me if I could help it. When I see what we now call bullying, even if it is different from what I observed during my early years, I feel utter disgust, but it does not just happen on a school playground or over the internet.

During my high school years, we all considered two girls to be the best of friends. Every day, they would stay together in the halls, classes, and after school. You could always find them together! I will call one of them Elizabeth (the leader and bully); the other one, I will call Alyce (the follower).

I saw Elizabeth get Alyce into all kinds of disturbing situations. Elizabeth would throw stones, hide her hands, and let Alyce take the blame for it.

Elizabeth would not defend Alyce when she got into trouble for something she had started. Others have told me that Elizabeth and Alyce were joined at the hip for many years until adulthood. Then, a tragic incident caused Alyce to finally realize that Elizabeth did not value her in their relationship. The Bible says, *"Bad company corrupts good character"* (1 Corinthians 15:33). I am sure you have seen relationships that suitably illustrate what the Bible is describing. They were far from healthy. In fact, they may have been very destructive. I have always been amazed at how

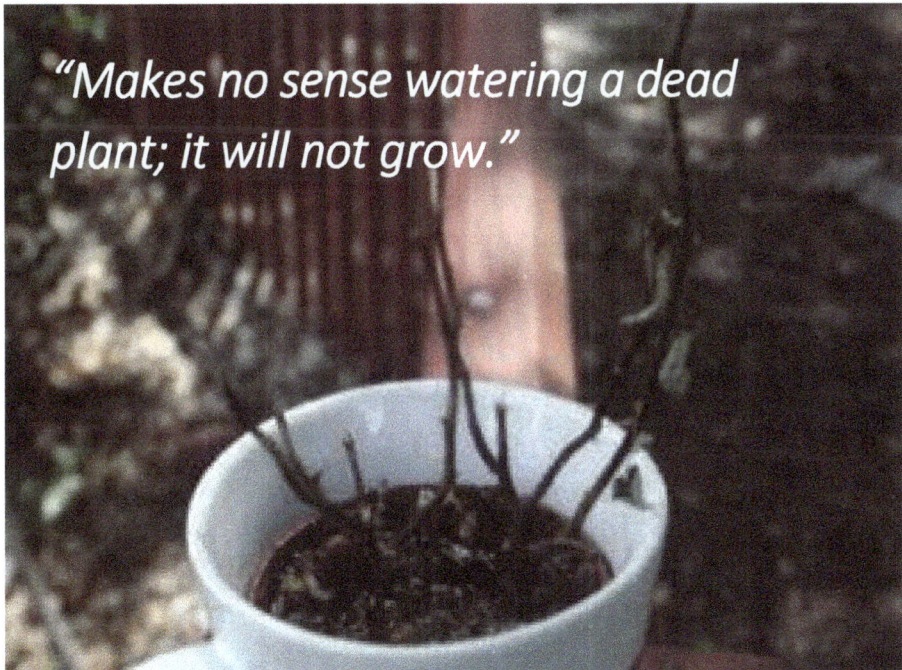

"Makes no sense watering a dead plant; it will not grow."

"Setting boundaries is a way of caring for myself. It doesn't make me mean, selfish or uncaring because I don't do things your way, I care about me too."

Unknown

really good women can get attracted and held captive by abusive relationships.

I have met lovely young women, with vibrant personalities, and a wholesome family background, who fell for a guy with an amazing bad streak. Understandably, she felt that she could change or "fix him." Even when the worst abuse happened, she was easy manipulated into believing that it was her fault. The abusive husband, lover, or friend convinces the victim that if she had not provoked his anger, she would not have been treated as though she was so worthless. Or, he would ask for forgiveness and shower her with gifts until she felt guilty for being so unforgiving and selfish.

It is important that you value others and yourself, and set boundaries. My mother used to tell me, "If you don't take care of yourself, no one else will." She would encourage me to watch out for others, but to also make sure I took care of myself. Unfortunately, in this life, many seek only self-gain.

Elizabeth had many people under her web of influence. Followers bowed to her every whim. Somehow, she convinced them that she was better than they were. It is crucial for you to learn that no one person is better than another. You have worth and value in the eyes of God. Therefore, you deserve as much respect as the next person. When you discover your real value on the inside, no one can take advantage of you.

When you are a winner on the inside, you can have winning relationships on the outside.

To build proper relationships, we must set realistic boundaries. Setting boundaries is how you care for yourself. Boundaries should not be set to keep us from developing healthy relationships or keep people out, but for encouraging the right relationships to form and grow. You cannot accept mistreatment or allow others to abuse you. Recognize your value and worth, because you have something special to offer.

Tanja Christine Jaeger said, "Define your boundaries and create your sacred space where you can be true to yourself." You need not be defensive about who you are because you are a little different from another person. We should celebrate our differences, and not conform to a societal classification of what is right or normal.

Knowing when and how to say "no," is crucial. Many do not know how to say "no." In so doing, they allow others to put them in difficult situations. Abuse can be physical and obvious, or it can be subtle and emotional. Either way, it is abuse, and we should never tolerate it. Say "no" early to establish and define the way you wish to be treated.

The Bible compares a woman to a beautiful kind of jewel – rubies (See Proverbs 31:10 and 3:15). Why is that? Rubies absorb light and are beautiful on the inside. When light shines through the red facets of a ruby, it brings beauty to others. Boundaries allow you to connect to others in healthy ways. Boundaries bring blessings.

Connecting to Others

"I guess when you're young; you just believe there'll be many people with whom you'll connect with. Later in life, you realize it only happens a few times" – Anonymous

God is the great connector! He joins together the proper alliances. Regardless of compatibility or not, our obligation is to connect people to God by our love and through prayer. Our duty is to treat others the way we wish to be treated.

Connecting is preferred but not required in all situations! Sometimes connecting with certain people cannot be done. Spiritual clashes are real, and some personalities simply cannot be balanced. I have met people who I, at first glance, could sense something in the spirit where we just clashed.

I remember the first time this happened to me. I was in elementary school. I got on the school bus, and as I looked at this certain little girl, we just collided in spirit. This very uneasy feeling came over me, and I had this feeling that I should stay away from this person. This was as a child. It happened again as an adult with another different person. The other person had done nothing to me, nor had I done anything to her.

As an adult, I saw this person often. We both thought the barrier between us was because we needed to get to know each other better. Therefore, we forced a meeting to talk with each other. We were not going to let the devil have a place in our lives.

However, it was not the devil. We just did not connect. No matter what we tried, we just were not meant to be friends. Sometimes there is no clashing, colliding, or uncomfortable feelings. Sometimes we just have a lack of affinity, no matter how much we care.

We should not waste time on those who do not show us mutual respect. Sometimes you can give people everything they claim to want, but it will never be enough. Even family members can be challenging. Although connected by blood, sometimes we are unable to establish healthy emotional and spiritual connections with others. Not all children bond with their parents. We should not exhaust our energy on meaningless friendships, forced interactions, or fruitless conversations. Such interactions only lead to drama. They never resolve issues because the issues do not exist. It is just a block between people.

Dwelling in the past ruins present relationships and jeopardizes what the future holds.

My oldest daughter always loved hard and put herself 100% into relationships with others. I considered some of her friends and acquaintances to be shallow and jealous. I often wondered, who was raising these children to befriend others for what they had, or could give (birthday presents, babysitting, etc.). They seemed incapable of being genuine people who cared about others. They had difficulty connecting because they lacked real integrity and authenticity. Also, my daughter had a few little quirks that made her different. I always encouraged her to associate with people who would value and celebrate her for who she was, and not try to make her into something she wasn't. I told her she marched to the beat of a different drummer and that was ok. Henry David Thoreau said, "If a man does not keep pace with his companions, perhaps it is because he hears a different drummer. Let him step to the music which he hears however measured or far away."

In life, we must eventually let go of all the pointless drama, and the people who create them. That time should be now because our time on this planet is short, no matter how long you live. People who make you laugh hard, the ones who are genuine, and those who are honest, are individuals you should allow into your space. You should forget the bad, and focus solely on the good. After all, life is too short to be anything but joyful, regardless of the situations and circumstances you experience.

Connecting is great when it happens naturally. It won't always happen that way though, and you will then have to work on your relationships with people. Connecting requires skill, but you can learn how. However, never compromise your self-esteem, self-worth, or your joy in the process. John Maxwell said, "Many communicate, but few connect."

It is true that the Bible tells us to love our enemies, but that does not essentially mean that we should encourage them to mistreat us or others. It does not mean that we should enable them to pursue a lifestyle that exposes us to danger. It may mean that we need to establish some safe distance between us and them.

During a certain period, King Saul had imagined that David was his enemy and sought to kill him. At one point, David had the opportunity to kill Saul, but he spared his life. That brought King Saul to a temporary repentance that he admitted how wrong he had been.

David apparently did forgive him, but it is important to notice that David did not return with Saul to his home. He went the opposite direction (See 1 Samuel 24:10-22). What does that mean for us? We can forgive those who have mistreated us, but we may still need to keep our distance from them. Certainly, that is the advice many abused wives and children need to hear. It is also what many adults need to understand when they recognize that they are involved in a destructive relationship.

Set your boundary and maintain it.

Set Healthy Boundaries

If you have set healthy boundaries, you will take responsibility for your own life and your own decisions. You will also allow others the same privilege. Boundaries allow us to make sacrifices for the benefit of others when it is appropriate, but not in a way that encourages them to be self-indulgent or overly demanding. This means that we should be open to meeting the needs of others when they cannot fulfill those needs on their own, but we should not sacrifice ourselves to fulfill their selfish desires. God meets our genuine needs, but that does not mean He wants to meet every whim we have.

If we give people a blank check to draw away all our emotional, mental, and financial reserves, we are making them cripples who will despise us when we can no longer satisfy their desires. Be careful. Many people say "yes" to the demands of others for fear of being rejected by them. That is a false kindness that is not motivated by real love.

The Bible, on numerous occasions, addresses the problem of the "fear of man;" even saying that it is a trap. It you live in fear of the disapproval of others, you are not free to make your own choices. You develop an unhealthy dependence on them that weakens your confidence and self-esteem.

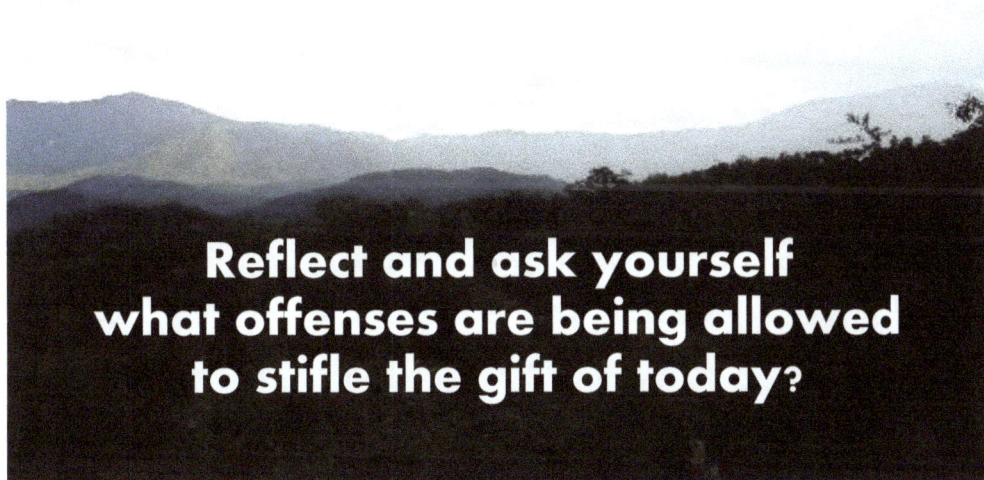

Reflect and ask yourself what offenses are being allowed to stifle the gift of today?

Boundaries show respect for others, as well as demonstrate our self-respect. They acknowledge that each of us is valuable, even if we are different. A friend who has his inner life in order isn't afraid to tell us the truth we need to hear, instead of a lie that would make us more comfortable (See Proverbs 27:6). Healthy boundaries are part of healthy relationships. When we respect one another's boundaries, it gives the freedom for us to love and serve one another, because our old nature is under control (See Galatians 5:13).

THE ANSWER IS
INSIDE

The Bible teaches that we have the mind of Christ (See 1 Corinthians 2:16). In the objective sense, that means we have access to the thoughts and the will of Christ through the Scriptures. However, we must not ignore the subjective truth available to us through the Spirit of Christ, who dwells within every true child of God (See Romans 8:9). He has been given to us as our constant Teacher and Guide (See John 14:26; 1 John 2:27).

The Scriptures and the Spirit are always in perfect harmony with one another, and each complements the other to guide our understanding as we seek to follow Him.

The Greater One Lives within Us

"Ye are of God, little children, and have overcome them: because greater is he that is in you, than he that is in the world."

1 John 4:4

The kingdom of God is within us, and the Scripture says that the Greater One lives within us (See Luke 17:21, 1 John 4:4). I remember the story of a young lady with whom I worked. She told me that she was a terrible person to deal with, and she was fired because of her bad attitude. After she got fired from her job, she spent some time evaluating her life. She considered who she was, why she was always so hostile, and why she treated others at work so badly. The way she treated her colleagues consequently provoked them to react against her. She needed answers for how to bring change to her life. She had begun to fall behind her peers, as she was not moving forward in many areas of her life.

Clearly, all was not going well for her. This is not who she wanted to be. That is why she set aside some time to look within and evaluate who she was and how she was behaving. She soon realized that her bad attitude was not getting her anywhere. She decided to make a change. Whether we like it or not, depending on God for all of our needs is imperative. *"He has designed us so that we need other people"* (Genesis 2:18). *"In the church, we have been made members of one another; all of us part of one body in Christ"* (See Romans 12:5, 1 Corinthians 12:27).

Avoid Planting Negative Actions

If you treat others badly, you are sure to be treated the same way in return. You should not expect any form of positive response from where you have planted negative actions. I was so astounded by the young lady's story.

Today, you too would be overwhelmed if you knew her. Indeed, the change in her life has been remarkable. She has grown to be a very lovely person, full of the love of Christ. Her life did not welcome a new touch until she examined herself. She did not become a woman full of life like she wanted, not until she looked inward to realize the basis for her terrible way of life.

Many of us have the same problem. We seek answers where they do not exist. We often believe too much of what life throws at us, instead of looking within and finding time to seek Him; the One who knows all. When we search for answers from the inside, we set ourselves on the right path to reconnecting with Him, the only One who can guide us wisely. We actually do have more answers than we can imagine; if we can just look deep within. Do not deny yourself of this peaceful reconciliation, where you can find answers to your problems by looking inward. You get the wrong answers simply because you wrongly rely on your brain, instead of the Spirit of the Lord that is within you. Our sufficiency is in Christ alone, not in ourselves. Joyce Meyer once said, "If your inner life is not producing what you would like on the outside, don't be discouraged... just be willing to change."

Use the Talents God Has Given You

You have only this one life. It would be a shame to not fully to use all the blessings God already provided. Remember the story of the servants who were given talents to use? One of the servants, who buried his gift so that it did not increase, could only return an undeveloped gift to his master. I beseech thee by the mercies of God, do not be like him!

Never allow the tribulations of this world to rob you of who you were originally designed to be. You have been given all you need to survive whatever experience you encounter.

Your community might not have the answers to your questions. The way other people find their answers will not necessarily be the best way for you to find yours. God has sent us a Comforter, the Holy Spirit. You should endeavor to have a genuine dialogue with Him at all times. You will find more answers there than you could ever find elsewhere.

The best thing about getting the answers from within is that they are the best answers.

Make Positive Affirmations

Positive affirmations will change the way you think and your perceptions on life. Constantly remind yourself of who you are, and try to walk in that consciousness. Post things on the mirror of your mind.

Tell yourself you are gifted, you are royal, and you are wonderfully and fearfully made in Christ. Knowing who you are, according to the Word of God, will help you to retrieve the correct answers from your heart when you look inside during life's challenges.

- You are a new creature (2 Cor. 5:17; cf. Gal. 5:6; 6:15; Eph. 2:10).

- You are a saint (1 Cor. 1:2).

- You are a part of His Church (Eph. 2:21-22).

- You are a temple for God's Spirit (Eph. 2:22).

- You are in the eternal plan of God (Eph. 1:4; 2 Tim. 1:9).

- You are complete and filled with the fullness of Christ (Col. 2:9).

- You are accepted (Eph. 1:6).

- You are secure in the love of God (Rom. 8:38-39).

- You are established, rooted and built up (2 Cor. 1:21; Col. 2:7).

- You are near to the heart of God (Eph. 2:13).

Know that you are beautiful, and have been made in the image and likeness of God.

You have the mind of God in all you do. If Christ indeed is the sculptor who molded you, you should never be dismayed because He will never forsake you. He has deposited in you all that is needed to make it in this world. Remember the Scripture states that we will never be tempted more than we can bear (See 1 Corinthians 10:13).

Henceforth, no matter what, always be conscious of who you are in Christ. Know that you are a unique creature, designed for a particular purpose. Never allow anyone to make you feel less worthy than you have been created to be. That however, also depends on your not treating anybody else with contempt. You are good enough. Rise above all those feelings of inadequacy. Believe in yourself, and always remind yourself of just how precious you are in the eyes of God. Meditate on the Scriptures, and find the answers you need from within. Unless the "within" is the Spirit of God, we can be deceived by our fleshly desires, even as Christians. It is important to be particularly clear about this because many young believers are not grounded well enough in the Word to recognize the difference.

Look Inside

God is the Artist and the Creator of everything. Everything He made is good. You are a chosen member of the royal priesthood, one who has a God-given purpose. God has placed a purpose and a destiny within you. Use every opportunity to be better at whom God has designed you to be, and look inside knowing that the answers lie within.

We go to counseling. We go to the coaches. We have everyone else looking for answers for our situation. But the answers actually are inside of us. Look inside!

The Scripture lets us know that if we keep our mind focused on God, He will keep us in perfect peace. (See Isaiah 26:3). Why will we have perfect peace? We have it because we trust in God, and do not allow external things to dictate who we are, and whose we are.

Hannah Whitall Smith said, "No soul can be really at rest until it has given up all dependence on everything else and has been forced to depend on the Lord alone. As long as our expectation is from other things, nothing but disappointment awaits us."

Have I arrived? Do I have it all together? No, but I have learned to wait before I speak and before I act.

You can save yourself frustrations and all kinds of problems when you evaluate your situations from the perspective of God. He made you, and He knows what is best for you. You do not have to be frustrated and confused trying to figure out "why" or "how."

When God places a period on a situation, you must not replace it with a question mark. We cannot always understand everything that happens to us, but there will come a time when God shall reveal things to us through the Scriptures, so that we may live a victorious life here on earth.

You should neither neglect having the Scriptures as your daily bread, nor the Spirit of Christ within you. Although we are insufficient in ourselves, we are made sufficient through these divine resources that enable us to walk in godliness, even in a fallen world.

I read this piece on an internet blog, Bibleinbits.Wordpress.com, on June 8, 2016. It was titled, *"A Word of Encouragement by* MRSMONI."[2] In the blog MRSMONI summed up much of what I have been espousing. It spoke to me regarding self-love, forgiving yourself and having a healthy self. Sometimes the enemy can be the devil, but when you genuinely look inside yourself, you can see that the enemy can be you. When we look in the mirror and honestly take a look inside, we can see we are at the heart of our joys and pain, or fears and failure, and triumphs, trials and tests.

---

[2] Whitehead, Monica D. "A Word of Encouragement for You." The Bible in Bits. June 8, 2016. https://bibleinbits.wordpress.com/2016/06/08/a-word-of-encouragement-for-you/.

Your perspective on life's challenges (good or bad) help to shape your outlook, self-image and your world view on how you see others. Your dealings with others are affected by how you deal with yourself and what you expect from yourself. Sometimes, we are harder on ourselves than we should be. We can be also be very hard on others because of who we are.

We are easily offended, but we also offend. We make excuses for ourselves but will not let others off the hook. How you treat yourself, how you allow others to treat you, and your relationship with God are all centered in our inner life – the relationship we have with ourselves.

In the blog, MRSMONI admits that she had some struggles because she did not look to God initially. She had an epiphany we must all learn to come to at some point. She was in a dark place. I was in a dark place, but the realization is one of understanding that the light is most appreciated in the midst of darkness.

The vow she asked us to take with her is poignant. It is reprinted here with her permission.

And so today, I vow to love myself, to be patient with myself, to forgive myself. I vow to believe that I am forgiven for all of the mistakes I have made in my past. I vow to see in myself, only things that are true and worthy of praise. I vow to admit my sins, repent, and turn to God. I vow to love others, unconditionally. I vow to listen and to only speak when asked. I vow to stop looking at and talking about the flaws I see in others. I vow to build up and not tear down. I vow to take off all of the pressure I put on myself and only put on the love that God has for me. I vow to be free so that others can see my freedom and wonder where it comes from. I vow to witness and attest that God is love and it is only love that has set me free.

Would you make this vow with me today? In the name of Jesus, Amen.

The only thing I would add to this vow is to look daily inside where the Holy Spirit resides, and vow to let Him lead and guide! The answers lie within. As we go through life, it will bring us tests and teach us lessons if we are prepared to learn them. There is no magic to living a full content life. We must reflect, evaluate, and assess what is on the inside, consistently clean up the junk, and lighten up, live and love.

Just like a computer, if we allow garbage in, we will get garbage out. Learn to hit the delete key to get rid of the viruses that affect our hard drives. A changed inside life can result in changed behavior in our outside life, making our relationships with others better. Realize you are a new creature, made in the image of God, old things have passed away.

DON'T YOU DARE GIVE UP!

About the Author

Terrie A. Alexander was born in Atlanta and has lived her fruitful life in this beautiful and flourishing city. She is a graduate of Murphy High School and Brenau College for Women, where she obtained a Bachelor's degree in Accounting.

Her business career has been both diverse and focused. After graduation from college, she began her ten-years of service with Wachovia Bank of Georgia. She rose to the position of Vice President of Retail Bank Audit Operations and Audit Manager. Since 1996, she has operated TARA Alexander, Inc. with her husband Ruben. Today, she is the Vice President of this thriving consulting company that offers diagnostic and staffing solution services. Beginning in 1998, and continuing to the present, she has been Secretary and Treasurer, Business Manager, and Human Resource Manager at Park Central Family Practice.

Since March 2016, Terrie has been a John Maxwell Team-Certified Coach, Trainer and Speaker. She is also a National Association of Professional Women nominee, and she was awarded the Trailblazer Leadership Award for the 13th Annual Celebration of Life Luncheon in 2015.

Terrie Alexander has served on two boards at Kaplan University, their Institutional Review Board and the University Advisory Board of their

Medical Assisting Program Nationwide. In addition, she has served as a Consultant and Guest Speaker for the Medical Assisting Program at Advanced Career Training.

Terrie served for ten years as the Financial Chair at Flat Shoals United Methodist Church from 1996-2006. She is on the Board of Directors of the Jimmie Lee Smith Community Center at Light of the World Christian Tabernacle in Stockbridge, Georgia.

Terrie is a licensed minister and has been devoted to ministry for many years. She was a Certified Lay Speaker for the United Methodist Church, Flat Shoals UMC. She was the Director of Christian Education for Light of the World Christian Tabernacle from 2011 through 2015. She has been the Women's Ministry President of LAMPS (Ladies Advancing Ministry through Praise and Service) since 2015.

Throughout her life, she has sought to balance family, community, and career. She has been remarkably successful in all three areas. She and her husband Ruben A. Alexander have been married for 34 years. Together, they have one son, a daughter in love, two daughters, and a beautiful granddaughter.

Contact Information

To contact Terrie A. Alexander for book signings or speaking engagements, please use the information below.

Terrie A. Alexander

https://www.linkedin.com/in/terrie-alexander

https://www.facebook.com/terrie.alexander.90

http://www.johncmaxwellgroup.com/terriealexander/

https://www.pinterest.com/nvpterrie/

www.ingramcontent.com/pod-product-compliance
Lightning Source LLC
Chambersburg PA
CBHW080519110426
42742CB00017B/3169